Golden Promises

Golden Promises

selected by Jo Petty

Published by The C. R. Gibson Company

Norwalk, Connecticut

According as his divine power that hath given unto us all things that pertain unto life and godliness, through knowledge of him that hath called us to glory and virtue:
Whereby are given unto us exceeding great and precious promises . . .

II Peter 1:3,4

Contents

This collection of favorite inspirational
passages from the Book of Books offers
guidance for everyday living.
While retaining the meaning of the
original King James version, many of
these profound yet familiar messages have
been paraphrased to speak more directly
to the reader. This personalized treasury
by one of America's most popular authors
will open new doors of faith and
understanding. Jo Petty, the compiler,
comments: "When I read the Bible, I feel
God is speaking directly to *me!*"

Love

God so loved the world, that He gave His only
begotten Son, that *whosoever* believeth in Him
should not perish, but have everlasting life.

If God so loved us, we ought also
to love one another.

Herein is love, not that *I* loved God,
but that He loved *me*, and sent His Son
to be the propitiation for *my* sins.

God sent not His Son into the world to
condemn the world; but that the world
through Him might be saved.

God forgives all *my* iniquities; He heals all *my*
diseases; He redeems *my* life from destruction;
He crowns *me* with lovingkindness and tender
mercies; He satisfies *my* mouth with good things,
so that *my* youth is renewed like the eagle's.

By love serve one another.

Grace be with all them that love our Lord
Jesus Christ in sincerity.

God will never leave me, nor forsake me.

Jesus came to seek and to save
those who are lost.

Behold, what manner of love the Father
has bestowed upon me.

The eternal God is my refuge, and underneath
are His everlasting arms.

Neither death, nor life, nor angels,
nor principalities, nor powers, nor things
present, nor things to come, nor height,
nor depth, nor any other creature, shall be able
to separate me from the love of God,
which is in Christ Jesus my Lord.

God has made of one blood all nations of men
for to dwell on all the face of the earth.

He that loves not knows not God; for God is love.

God will have all men to be saved, and to
come unto the knowledge of the truth.

Whoever comes to Jesus,
He will in no wise cast out.

Jesus is the true Light, who lights every
man that comes into the world.

The Lord has appeared of old unto me, saying,
Yea, I have loved you with an everlasting love:
therefore with lovingkindness have I drawn you.

Jesus was in the world, and the world was
made by Him, and the world knew Him not.

Love rejoices in truth.

Jesus came into the world to bear witness of the truth. If *I* am of the truth, *I* hear His voice.

Bless the Lord, O *my* soul: and all that is within *me*, bless His holy name.

Heaven and earth shall pass away: but Jesus' words shall not pass away.

If *I* continue in Jesus' words, *I* am His disciple indeed; and *I* shall know the truth, and the truth shall make *me* free.

Jesus calls *me* friend; for He has made known to *me* all things He heard of His Father.

We are more than conquerors, through Him that loved us.

Not every one who says Lord, Lord, shall enter into the kingdom of heaven; but he that does the will of our Father in heaven.

If *I* have not the Spirit of Christ, *I* am not His.

If *I* am led by the Spirit of God, *I* am His child and if a child, a joint-heir with Christ.

Wear a breastplate of faith and love; and for a helmet, the hope of salvation.

Why do *I* call Jesus Lord, Lord, if *I* do not the things which He says?

Jesus Christ is the author of eternal salvation unto all them that obey Him.

Now abides faith, hope, and love, but the greatest of these is love.

I shall love the Lord *my* God with all *my* heart,
and with all *my* soul, and with all *my* mind.
This is the first commandment. And the second is like,
namely this, *I* shall love *my* neighbor as *myself*.
There are no commandments greater than these.

If *I* set *my* love on God, He will answer *me*
when *I* call: He will be with *me* in trouble; He
will deliver *me*, and honor *me*. With long life
will He satisfy *me*, and show *me* His salvation.

Cast *me* not away from Your presence;
and take not Your Holy Spirit from *me*.
Restore unto *me* the joy of Your salvation
and uphold *me* with Your free Spirit.

I am not worthy of Christ if *I* love son or
daughter or father or mother more than *I* love Him.

God is love; and he that dwells in love
dwells in God, and God in him.

If *I* love God, *I* love my brother also.

Love in deed and in truth rather than in word.

If *I* have no compassion for *my* brother in
need, the love of God dwells not in *me*.

All things whatsoever *I* would that men should
do to *me*, I must do even so to them.

I must from *my* heart forgive
my brother his trespasses.

I should forgive *my* brother
seventy times seven.

If *I* love Jesus, *I* will keep His commandments.

Love works no ill to his neighbor: therefore
love is the fulfilling of the law.

He that says he is in the light, and
hates his brother is in darkness.

Mercy unto you, and peace, and love be multiplied.

Many waters cannot quench love,
neither can floods drown it.

We, being many, are one body in Christ, and
every one members one of another.

Love is the bond of everything perfect.

If we love one another, God dwells in us,
and His love is perfected in us.

Owe no man any thing, but to love one another:
for he who loves another has fulfilled the law.

If your enemy be hungry, give him bread to eat;
and if he be thirsty, give him water to drink.

If I love only those who love me,
what reward have I?

If I forgive not men their trespasses,
neither will my Father forgive my trespasses.

Whoso stops his ears at the cry of the poor, he
also shall cry himself, but shall not be heard.

Increase and abound in love one toward
another, and toward all men.

Love is of God; and everyone that loves is
born of God, and knows God.

God's word is truth.

If we have love one to another, all men will
know that we are Jesus' followers.

A friend loves at all times, and a brother
is born for adversity.

Greater love has no man than this, that a
man lay down his life for his friends.

If *I* love the world, the love of the Father
is not in *me*.

All that is in the world, the lust of the flesh,
and the lust of the eyes, and the pride of life,
is not of the Father, but is of the world . . .
but he that does the will of God abides for ever.

Love shall cover the multitude of sins.

Love thinks no evil.

Love is not easily provoked.

Love is not selfish.

Love never fails.

Love does not brag or boast of self.

Love does not envy.

Love suffers long and is kind.

Love endures all things.

If *I* hear Jesus' sayings and do them, *I*
shall be like a wise man, who built his house
upon a rock: and the rain descended, and
the floods came, and the winds blew, and
beat upon his house; and it fell not: for
it was founded on a rock.

A man who has many friends
must show himself friendly.

There is a friend that sticketh closer
than a brother.

Forget not to entertain strangers: for
thereby some have entertained angels unawares.

I must honor the Lord with my substance, and with
the firstfruits of all my increase.

Support the weak and cheer the fainthearted.

The price of a virtuous woman is far above
rubies. The heart of her husband safely trusts
in her. She will do him good and not evil all
the days of her life. Strength and honor are
her clothing; and she shall rejoice in time to
come. She opens her mouth with wisdom; and in
her tongue is the law of kindness. She eats
not the bread of idleness. Her children arise
up, and call her blessed; her husband also, and
he praises her. Many daughters have done
virtuously, but she excels them all.

I should therefore be merciful
as my Father also is merciful.

Be ye therefore followers of God, as dear
children; and walk in love.

To whom little is forgiven, the same loves little.

We that are strong ought to bear the infirmities
of the weak, and not to please ourselves.

I must not put a stumbling block or an
occasion to fall in my brother's way.

Weep with them that weep and rejoice
with them that do rejoice.

Remember the poor.

If *I* forgive, *I* shall be forgiven.

If *I* judge not and condemn not,
I shall not be judged nor condemned.

The unbelieving husband is sanctified by the
wife, and the unbelieving wife is sanctified
by the husband. . .

Children should obey their parents for
this is well pleasing unto the Lord.

Foolishness is bound in the heart of a
child; but the rod of correction shall
drive it far from him.

He that spares his rod hates his son: but
he that loves him chastens him.

In heaven the angels of the little ones do always
behold the face of our Father in heaven.

It is not the will of our Father in heaven
that one of these little ones should perish.

In order that it may be well with *me*
and that *I* might live long on the earth,
I must honor my father and mother.

He that loveth silver shall not be satisfied with
silver; nor he that loveth abundance with increase.

The end of the commandment is love
out of a pure heart, and of a good
conscience, and of faith unfeigned.

There is no fear in love;
but perfect love casteth out fear.

God has not given me the spirit of fear; but
of power, and of love, and of a sound mind.

He who keeps His word, in him is
the love of God perfected.

He that has pity upon the poor lends unto the Lord;
and that which he has given will He pay him again.

God's tender mercies and lovingkindnesses
have been ever of old.

I am poor and needy; yet the Lord thinks of me!

The angel of the Lord encamps round about
them that fear Him, and delivers them.

God is a father of the fatherless
and a judge of the widows.

In Thee, O Lord, do I put my trust:
Cast me not off in the time of old age;
forsake me not when my strength fails.

Even to your old age I am God; and even to hoar
hairs will I carry you: I have made, and I will
bear; even I will carry and deliver you.

Jesus came that I might have life and that I
might have it more abundantly.

I love the Lord, because He hath heard my voice
and my supplications.

God has commanded me to keep His
precepts diligently.

Joy

Let us come before His presence with thanksgiving,
and make a joyful noise unto Him with psalms.

Jesus Christ is the same yesterday,
and today, and for ever.

By the word of the Lord were the heavens made; and
all the host of them by the breath of His mouth.

The heavens declare the glory of God; and the
firmament shows His handiwork. Day unto day
utters speech, and night unto night shows
knowledge. There is no speech nor language
where their voice is not heard.

The Lord reigneth; let the earth rejoice.

The joy of the Lord is *my* strength.

Holy, holy, holy, is the Lord of hosts: the
whole earth is full of His glory.

Blessed be God, even the Father of our
Lord Jesus Christ, the Father of mercies,
and the God of all comfort.

Blessed is the nation whose God is the Lord.

Those who love God's Name shall be joyful in Him.

Let all those that put their trust in God
rejoice: let them ever shout for joy, because
God defends them.

Blessed is everyone that fears the Lord,
that walks in His ways. He shall eat
the labor of his hands, happy shall he be,
and it shall be well with him.

Serve the Lord with gladness: come before His
presence with singing.

Great is the Lord, and greatly to be praised.

From the rising of the sun unto the going down
of the same the Lord's name is to be praised.

Praise the Lord for His goodness, and for
His wonderful works to the children of men.

Sacrifice the sacrifice of thanksgiving, and
declare God's works with rejoicing.

I was glad when they said unto *me*,
Let us go into the house of the Lord.

Give unto the Lord the glory due unto His name.

One generation shall praise God's works to
another, and shall declare His mighty acts.

Thou hast turned *my* mourning into dancing: Thou
hast put off *my* sackcloth, and girded *me* with
gladness; to the end that *my* glory may sing praise
to Thee, and not be silent. O Lord my God, *I* will
give thanks unto Thee for ever.

Come and hear, all that fear God, and *I*
will declare what He has done for *my* soul.

I was as a sheep going astray; but am now
returned unto the Shepherd.

Only fear the Lord, and serve Him in truth
with all your heart: for consider how great
things He has done for you.

Blessed are they that hear the word
of God, and keep it.

But thanks be to God, which giveth us the
victory through our Lord Jesus Christ.

God's word is a lamp unto *my* feet, and a
light unto *my* path.

God's testimonies have *I* taken as a heritage for
ever: for they are the rejoicing of *my* heart.

I will sing unto the Lord, because He has
dealt bountifully with *me*.

God has crowned man with glory and honor.
Man was made to have dominion over the
works of God's hand.

God is light.

For God, who commanded the light to shine
out of darkness, has shined in our hearts,
to give the light of knowledge of the
glory of God in the face of Jesus Christ.

I will offer sacrifices of joy; *I* will sing,
yea, *I* will sing praises unto the Lord.

God's yoke is easy, and His burden is light.

The hope of the righteous shall be gladness: but the expectation of the wicked shall perish.

The blessing of the Lord, it makes rich, and He adds no sorrow with it.

In God's presence is fulness of joy and pleasures for evermore.

The prayer of the upright is God's delight.

With God is the fountain of life: in His light *I* shall see light.

If *I* ask in Jesus' Name, *I* shall receive, that *my* joy may be full.

In Thee, O Lord, do *I* put my trust.

Blessed be the Lord God . . . only He does wondrous things.

Rejoice in the Lord alway.

Rejoice in hope.

Great is *my* Lord, and of great power: His understanding is infinite.

This is the day which the Lord has made; *I* will rejoice and be glad in it.

O give thanks unto the Lord; call upon His name: make known His deeds among the people.

. . . Stand still, and consider the wondrous works of God.

These things have I spoken unto you, that My joy might remain in you, and that your joy might be full.

O taste and see that the Lord is good:
blessed is the man that trusts in Him.

Worship the Lord in the beauty of holiness.

O Lord, open Thou *my* lips; and *my* mouth
shall show forth Thy praise.

Light is sown for the righteous, and gladness for
the upright in heart.

Whoso trusts in the Lord, happy is he.

God has put gladness in *my* heart.

What shall *I* give back to the Lord for all
His benefits toward *me*?

God loves a cheerful giver.

In every thing give thanks: for this is the
will of God in Christ Jesus concerning *me*.

Rejoice evermore.

The Lord has done great things for *me*;
whereof *I* am glad.

I will greatly rejoice in the Lord, *my* soul
shall be joyful in *my* God: for He has clothed
me with the garments of salvation.

The Lord is *my* strength and *my* shield; *my* heart
trusts in Him, and *I* am helped: therefore
my heart greatly rejoices; and with *my* song
will *I* praise Him.

Joy shall be in heaven over one sinner that
repents, more than over ninety and nine just
persons who need no repentance.

Hope deferred makes the heart sick: but when
the desire comes, it is a tree of life.

Praise Him for His mighty acts: praise Him
according to His excellent greatness.

Incline your ear, and come to God: hear, and
your soul shall live.

Heaviness in the heart of man makes it
stoop: but a good word makes it glad.

They who sow in tears shall reap in joy.

He who goes forth and weeps, bearing precious
seed, shall doubtless come again with rejoicing,
bringing his sheaves with him.

I will praise Thee: for I am fearfully
and wonderfully made.

God gives more grace.

O magnify the Lord with me, and let us
exalt His name together.

Great is my reward in heaven if I am persecuted
for righteousness' sake, and I should
rejoice and be exceedingly glad.

I have trusted in God's mercy; my heart
shall rejoice in His salvation.

My joy no man takes from me.

In the world we shall have tribulation: but be
of good cheer; Jesus has overcome the world.

Serve the Lord with gladness.

Go out with joy, and be led forth with peace.

Every creature of God is good, and nothing
to be refused, if it be received with
thanksgiving: For it is sanctified by the
word of God and prayer.

Go your way, eat your bread with joy, and
drink your wine with a merry heart; for God
now accepts your works.

Live joyfully with the wife you love all
the days of your life, for that is your
portion in this life, and in your labor.

It is a good thing to give thanks unto the Lord,
and to sing praises unto His name, to show forth
His lovingkindness in the morning, and His
faithfulness every night.

God makes the outgoings of the morning and
evening to rejoice.

O give thanks unto the Lord; for He is good:
because His mercy endures for ever.

The Lord is my strength and song,
and is my salvation.

God gives me richly all things to enjoy.

There is nothing better for a man, than
that he should eat and drink, and that he
should make his soul enjoy good in his
labor. . . . This is from the hand of God.

Let the word of Christ dwell in you richly in all
wisdom; teaching and admonishing one another in
psalms and hymns and spiritual songs, singing
with grace in your hearts to the Lord.

Peace

If *I* let *my* moderation be known unto all men and
if *I* am careful for nothing; but in every thing by
prayer and supplication with thanksgiving let *my*
requests be known unto God, then the peace of God,
which passes all understanding, shall keep
my heart and mind through Christ Jesus.

Mark the perfect man, and behold the upright:
for the end of that man is peace.

Come to Jesus, all *you* who labor and are heavy laden,
and He will give *you* rest.

God is not the author of confusion, but of peace.

If it be possible, . . . live peaceably with all men.

Godliness with contentment is great gain.

Whoso puts his trust in the Lord shall be safe.

Length of days, and long life, and peace, shall be
added to whoever keeps God's commandments.

Whoso hearkens unto the Lord shall dwell safely,
and shall be quiet from fear of evil.

Anger rests in the bosom of fools.

The sleep of a laboring man is sweet,
whether he eat little or much.

Great peace have they who love God's law:
and nothing shall offend them.

Cast all your care upon God; for He cares for you.

The peacemakers shall be called the children of God.

God will keep him in perfect peace, whose mind
is stayed on Him: because he trusts in God.

No man is able to pluck me out of my Father's hand.

. . . Live in peace; and the God of love and peace
shall be with you.

In God I have put my trust; I will not fear
what flesh can do to me.

God sets fast the mountains; He stills the noise
of the seas, the noise of the waves, and the
tumult of the people.

In times when I am afraid, I will trust in God.

Every city or house divided against itself
shall not stand.

Except I be born of water and of the Spirit,
I cannot enter into the kingdom of God. That
which is born of the flesh is flesh; and that
which is born of the Spirit is spirit. I must
be born again. The wind blows where it lists,
and I hear the sound thereof, but cannot tell
whence it comes, and whither it goes: so is every
one that is born of the Spirit.

I will both lay *me* down in peace, and sleep:
for Thou, Lord, only makest *me* dwell in safety.

Let us therefore follow after the things
which make for peace.

The Lord is *my* helper, and *I* will not fear
what man shall do unto *me*.

Be content with such things as *you* have.

How will *I* profit if *I* gain the whole world,
and lose *my* own soul?

Wars and fightings come even of our lusts
that war in our members.

Fulfil *my* joy, that *you* be likeminded, having
the same love, being of one accord, of one mind.

Where envying and strife is,
there is confusion and every evil work.

We should be at peace among ourselves.

Supplications, prayers, intercessions,
and giving of thanks, should be made for all men;
for kings, and for all that are in authority;
that we may lead a quiet and peaceable life
in all godliness and honesty.

They that take the sword
shall perish with the sword.

Better is a handful of quietness than both
hands full with travail and vexation of spirit.

It is vain for *me* to rise up early, to sit up
late, to eat the bread of sorrows: for so the
Lord gives His beloved sleep.

Follow peace with all men.

In the multitude of counsellors there is safety.

The fear of the wicked shall come upon him:
but the desire of the righteous shall be granted.

As one whom his mother comforteth,
so will God comfort you.

The wicked are like the troubled sea . . . it cannot
rest, whose waters cast up mire and dirt. There
is no peace, saith my God to the wicked.

When my ways please the Lord, He makes even
my enemies to be at peace with me.

The discretion of a man defers his anger; and it
is his glory to pass over a transgression.

The fear of the Lord is a guide to life:
and he who has it shall abide satisfied;
he shall not be visited with evil.

It is better to dwell in the wilderness,
than with a contentious and an angry woman.

A prudent man forsees the evil, and hides himself:
but the simple pass on and are punished.

We beseech you to study to be quiet, and to do your
own business, and to work with your own hands.

Let the peace of God rule in my heart
and be thankful.

I may be troubled on every side, yet not
distressed; I may be perplexed, but not in
despair; persecuted, but not forsaken;
cast down, but not destroyed.

The soul of the man that fears the Lord shall dwell
at ease; and his seed shall inherit the earth.

I shall not fear nor be afraid, for the Lord is
my light and my salvation.

God is my refuge and strength, a very present
help in trouble. Therefore, I will not fear,
though the earth be removed, and though the
mountains be carried into the midst of the sea.

God is my hiding place; He shall preserve me
from trouble; He shall compass me about with
songs of deliverance.

Fret not *thyself* because of evildoers.

God hides *me* under the shadow of His wings.

There is no want to them that fear God.

If *I* desire life, and love many days, that *I*
may see good, I will keep my tongue from evil,
and my lips from speaking guile. *I* will depart
from evil and do good; seek peace and pursue it.

Peace I leave with *you*, My peace I give unto *you*.

Patience

Let *me* run with patience the race
that is set before *me*.

Better is the end of a thing than the beginning
thereof: and the patient in spirit is better than
the proud in spirit.

Have mercy upon *me*, O God, according to Thy
lovingkindness: according to the multitude of
Thy tender mercies blot out *my* transgressions.

Bless the Lord, O *my* soul,
and forget not all His benefits:
Who forgives all *my* iniquities;
who heals all *my* diseases.

Why am *I* cast down, and why am *I* disquieted
within? *I* shall hope in God and shall yet
praise Him, Who is the health of *my* countenance.

Many are the afflictions of the righteous:
but the Lord delivereth him out of them all.

God heals the broken in heart,
and binds up their wounds.

In my distress *I* called to the Lord, and cried
to my God: He heard my voice, . . . and my cry came
before Him, even into His ears.

The rock of my strength, and my refuge, is in God.

Despise not the chastening of the Lord;
nor be weary of His correction:
for whom the Lord loves He corrects;
even as a father the son in whom he delights.

As many as God loves, He rebukes and chastens.

For a small moment has God forsaken me; but with
great mercies will He gather me. In a little
wrath He hid His face from me for a moment; but
with everlasting kindness will He have mercy on
me, says the Lord my Redeemer.

When *I* pass through the waters, God will be with
me; and through the rivers, they shall not overflow
me, when *I* walk through the fire, *I* shall not
be burned; neither shall the flame kindle upon me.

Take refuge in the shadow of God's wings until
your calamities are overpast.

God has not despised nor abhorred the affliction
of the afflicted; neither has He hid His face
from him; but when he cried unto God, He heard.

The salvation of the righteous is of the Lord:
He is their strength in the time of trouble.

The Lord also will be a refuge for the oppressed,
a refuge in times of trouble.

I must through much tribulation
enter into the kingdom of God.

He that endures to the end shall be saved.

He will regard the prayer of the destitute,
and not despise their prayer.

We glory in tribulations also: knowing that
tribulation works patience; And patience,
experience; and experience, hope.

Be patient toward all men.

Father, if it be possible, remove this cup from
me: nevertheless not my will, but Thine be done.

A prophet is not without honour, but in his
own country, and among his own kin, and in
his own house.

All that will live godly in Christ Jesus
shall suffer persecution.

I am blessed if I endure temptation: for when I
am tried, I shall receive the crown of life, which
the Lord has promised to them that love Him.

When the enemy shall come in like a flood,
the Spirit of the Lord shall lift up a
standard against him.

If I faint in the day of adversity,
my strength is small.

I should gladly glory in my infirmities,
that the power of Christ may rest on me . . .
for when I am weak, then am I strong.

My light affliction, which is but for a moment,
works for me a far more exceeding and eternal
weight of glory.

Blessed is he that considers the poor: the Lord
will deliver him in time of trouble. The Lord
will strengthen him on the bed of languishing.

Wait on the Lord, be of good courage, and He
will strengthen your heart.

God shows me great and sore troubles, but He shall
quicken me again, and shall bring me up again from
the depths of the earth.

The Lord is righteous in all His ways,
and holy in all His works.

I know that, whatsoever God does, it shall
be for ever: nothing can be put to it,
nor anything taken from it: and God does
it, that men should fear before Him.

I have set the Lord always before me: because
He is at my right hand, I shall not be moved.

God saves those who put their trust in Him from
those that rise up against them.

He who gathers in summer is a wise son: but he
that sleeps in harvest is a son that causes shame.

The needy shall not always be forgotten.

God is the helper of the fatherless.

Rest in the Lord, and wait patiently for Him.

God's anger endures but a moment; in His favor is
life: Weeping may endure for a night, but joy
comes in the morning.

I have need of patience, that, after I have done
the will of God, I might receive the promise.

The thing which has been, it is that which
shall be; and that which is done is that which
shall be done.

The way of transgressors is hard.

God is longsuffering and not willing that
any should perish, but that all should come
to repentance.

It is good for me that I have been afflicted;
that I might learn God's statutes.

Unless God's law had been my delight, I should
have perished in my affliction.

It is good that I should both hope and quietly
wait for the salvation of the Lord.

Though the Lord cause grief, yet
will He have compassion
according to the multitude of His mercies.

God does not afflict willingly nor grieve the
children of men.

Despise not the chastening of the Lord,
nor faint when you are rebuked of Him:
for whom the Lord loves He chastens,
and scourges every one He receives.

No chastening for the present seems to be joyous,
but grievous: nevertheless afterward it yields
the peaceable fruit of righteousness unto them
who are exercised thereby.

When Jesus was reviled, He reviled not again;
when He suffered, He threatened not; but
committed Himself to Him who judges righteously.

Forsake not the assembling of ourselves together,
but exhort one another.

I must keep my heart with all diligence; for out
of it come the issues of life.

The Lord upholds all that fall, and raises
up all those that be bowed down.

If I do well, and suffer for it, and take it
patiently, this is acceptable with God.

Murmur not.

Be not weary in well doing: for in due season
you shall reap, if you faint not.

Be patient in tribulation.

Bless those who persecute me.

Recompense to no man evil for evil.

Avenge not yourself, . . . vengeance is the Lord's.

They that wait upon the Lord shall renew their
strength; they shall mount up with wings as
eagles; they shall run, and not be weary;
and they shall walk, and not faint.

Fools because of their transgressions, and because
of their iniquities, are afflicted. Their soul
abhors all manner of meat; and they draw near unto
the gates of death. Then they cry unto the Lord in
their trouble, and He saves them out of their
distresses. He sends His word, and heals them, and
delivers them from their destruction.

The patient in spirit is better than
the proud in spirit.

When *I* suffer according to the will of God,
I should commit the keeping of *my* soul to God
in well doing, as unto a faithful Creator.

If anyone compels *you* to go a mile, go with him two.

Turn not away from him who would borrow of *me*.

Love *your* enemies, bless them that curse *you*,
do good to them that hate *you*.

Pray for them who despitefully use *you*
and persecute *you*.

If *I* forgive men their trespasses, *my* heavenly
Father will forgive *me*.

Follow after righteousness, godliness, faith,
love, patience, meekness.

Give strong drink unto him that is ready to
perish, and wine unto those that be of heavy
hearts. Let him drink, and forget his poverty,
and remember his misery no more.

Overcome evil with good.

Judge nothing before the time, until the Lord
come, who both will bring to light the hidden
things of darkness, and will make manifest the
counsels of the hearts: and then shall every
man have praise of God.

Men ought always to pray, and not to faint.

God will not suffer *me* to be tempted above that
which *I* am able to bear; but will with the
temptation also make a way to escape, that
I may be able to bear it.

Goodness

The eyes of the Lord are in every place
beholding the evil and the good.

God will render glory, honour, and peace,
to every man that worketh good.

God has made Jesus, Who knew no sin, to
be sin for me; that I might be made the
righteousness of God in Him.

God's faithfulness is to all generations.

While the earth remaineth, seedtime and
harvest, and cold and heat, and summer and
winter, and day and night shall not cease.

He that diligently seeks good procures favor.

God is no respecter of persons: but in
every nation he that fears God and works
righteousness is accepted with Him.

This I recall to my mind, therefore I have hope.
It is of the Lord's mercies that we are not
consumed, because His compassions fail not.

Not he who commends himself is approved,
but whom the Lord commends.

Cast away from me all *my* transgressions;
and make *me* a new heart and a new spirit.

Learn to do well; seek judgment,
relieve the oppressed, judge the fatherless,
plead for the widow.

He has shown *you*, O man, what is good;
and what the Lord requires of *you*:
that *you* do justly, and love mercy,
and walk humbly with *your* God.

Come now, and let us reason together, says
the Lord: though *my* sins be as scarlet,
they shall be white as snow; though they be
red like crimson, they shall be as wool.

God's word have *I* hid in *my* heart that *I* might
not sin against Him.

Seven things are an abomination to the Lord:
A proud look,
A lying tongue,
Hands that shed innocent blood,
A heart that devises wicked imaginations,
Feet that be swift in running to mischief,
A false witness that speaks lies,
And he that sows discord among brethren.

Withhold not good from them to whom it is due,
when it is in the power of *your* hand to do it.

Though hand join in hand, the wicked shall
not be unpunished; but the seed of the
righteous shall be delivered.

Godliness is profitable unto all things,
having promise of the life that now is,
and of that which is to come.

Remove not the ancient landmark,
which *your* fathers have set.

The righteous is delivered out of trouble.

Riches profit not in the day of wrath: but
righteousness delivers from death.

A false balance is abomination to the Lord:
but a just weight is His delight.

The fear of the Lord prolongs days: but the
years of the wicked shall be shortened.

The hope of the righteous shall be gladness.

He who walks uprightly walks surely.

The labour of the righteous tends to life;
the fruit of the wicked to sin.

In the way of righteousness is life; and in
the pathway thereof there is no death.

Lying lips are abomination to the Lord:
but they that deal truly are His delight.

The steps of a good man are ordered by the
Lord: and the Lord delights in his way.

He who gets riches and not by right, shall
leave them in the midst of his days, and at
his end shall be a fool.

Honour *thy* father and *thy* mother: that *thy*
days may be long upon the land which the
Lord *thy* God giveth *thee*.

Jesus came to call sinners to repentance.

Evil pursues sinners: but to the righteous
good shall be repayed.

Let the wicked forsake his way and the
unrighteous man his thoughts: and let
him return unto the Lord, and He will
have mercy upon him; and to our God, for
He will abundantly pardon.

A good man obtains favour of the Lord: but a
man of wicked devices will He condemn.

The wicked borrows, and pays not again: but
the righteous shows mercy and gives.

Treasures of wickedness profit nothing: but
righteousness delivers from death.

The Lord will not suffer the soul of the
righteous to famish: but He casts away
the substance of the wicked.

Let your love be sincere. Abhor that which
is evil; cleave to that which is good.

He who hastens to be rich has an evil eye,
and considers not that poverty shall come upon him.

The just man falls seven times, and
rises up again: but the wicked shall
fall into mischief.

The candle of the wicked shall be put out.

You shall not respect persons in judgment;
but you shall hear the small as well as the
great; . . . for the judgment is God's.

The just man walks in his integrity;
his children are blessed after him.

Even a child is known by his doings, whether
his work be pure, and whether it be right.

Every way of man is right in his own eyes;
but the Lord ponders the hearts.

He also that is slothful in his work is
brother to him that is a great waster.

The Lord is far from the wicked: but He
heareth the prayer of the righteous.

The hoary head is a crown of glory, if it
be found in the way of righteousness.

A whisperer separates chief friends.

He who walks with wise men shall be wise:
but a companion of fools shall be destroyed.

A good man leaves an inheritance to his children's
children: and the wealth of the sinner is
laid up for the just.

Go from the presence of a foolish man, when
you perceive not in him the lips of knowledge.

He that despises his neighbor sins:
but he that has mercy on the poor,
happy is he.

In Christ *I* have redemption through His
blood, even the forgiveness of sins.

He who covers his sins shall not prosper:
but whoso confesses and forsakes them
shall have mercy.

Oh how great is God's goodness, which He
has laid up for them that fear Him; which
He has wrought for them that trust in Him
before the sons of men.

The earth is full of the goodness of the Lord.

The righteous cry, and the Lord hears, and
delivers them out of all their troubles.

The face of the Lord is against them
that do evil.

The eyes of the Lord are upon the righteous,
and His ears are open unto their cry.

Remember not the sins of my youth,
nor my transgressions:
according to Thy mercy remember
Thou me for Thy goodness' sake, O Lord.

Order my conversation aright and I shall
see the salvation of God.

To show favoritism among persons is not
good: because for a piece of bread that
man will transgress.

He who makes haste to be rich
shall not be innocent.

The law of the Lord is perfect, converting
the soul: the testimony of the Lord is sure,
making wise the simple.

The eyes of the Lord are over the righteous,
and His ears are open unto their prayers:
but the face of the Lord is against them
that do evil.

God's way is perfect.

Every good tree brings forth good fruit;
but a corrupt tree brings forth evil fruit.

Let not presumptuous sins
have dominion over *me*.

Cleanse Thou *me*, O God, from secret faults.

Better is a little with righteousness than
great revenues without right.

By the fear of the Lord men depart from evil.

Let *me* search and try *my* ways, and turn
again to the Lord.

Lay aside all malice, and all guile,
and hypocrisies, and envies,
and all evil speakings.

If *I* know to do good, and do it not,
I have sinned.

If *my* eye is good, *my* whole body shall be
full of light. If *my* eye be evil, *my* whole
body shall be full of darkness.

The path of the just is as the shining light,
that shines more and more unto the perfect day.

Speak not evil one of another.

Out of the same mouth proceeds blessing and
cursing. With *my* tongue bless *I* God and
curse *I* men, who are made after the similitude
of God. These things ought not so to be.

By *my* words *I* shall be justified, and by *my*
words *I* shall be condemned.

Feed the hungry, give drink to the thirsty,
take into *your* home the strangers, clothe
the naked, visit the sick and those in prison.
Inasmuch as *we* do this unto the least of
our brothers, *we* do it unto Jesus.

O praise the Lord . . . all ye people. For His
merciful kindness is great toward us: and
the truth of the Lord endureth for ever.

Prove all things; hold fast that which is good.

Ever follow that which is good to all men.

Render not evil for evil unto any man.

Not by works of righteousness which
I have done, but according to His mercy
He saved *me*.

The Lord is good unto them that wait for Him,
to the soul that seeks Him.

Pure religion and undefiled before God is this,
to visit the fatherless and widows in
their affliction, and to keep *myself*
unspotted from the world.

Be a doer of the word, and not a hearer
only, deceiving *yourself*.

Be swift to hear, slow to speak,
slow to wrath: for the wrath of man
works not the righteousness of God.

I am tempted when *I* am drawn away by *my* own
lust, and enticed.

Out of the abundance of the heart
the mouth speaketh.

Hear *me*, O Lord; for Thy lovingkindness
is good: turn unto *me* according to the
multitude of Thy tender mercies.

Render therefore unto Caesar the things
which are Caesar's; and unto God the
things that are God's.

Take heed not to let any root of
bitterness spring up and trouble *you*,
and thereby many be defiled.

Except *I* be converted, and become as a
little child, *I* shall not enter into
the kingdom of heaven.

Thou openest Thine hand, and satisfieth the
desire of every living thing.

Let not mercy and truth forsake *you*:
bind them about *your* neck;
write them on the table of *your* heart.

My communication should be yea, yea; nay,
nay; for whatever is more comes of evil.

I cannot serve two masters.

The son shall not bear the iniquity of the
father, neither shall the father bear the
iniquity of the son: the righteousness of
the righteous shall be upon him, and the
wickedness of the wicked shall be upon him.

If a man be just, and do that which is lawful
and right . . . , he shall surely live.

All souls are God's: . . . the soul that sins,
it shall die.

The Lord will bless the righteous; with favor
will He compass him as with a shield.

Good and upright is the Lord: therefore
will He teach sinners in the way.

The Lord is good and ready to forgive;
and plenteous in mercy unto all them
who call upon Him.

Offer the sacrifices of righteousness,
and put *your* trust in the Lord.

He that walks uprightly, and works
righteousness, and speaks the truth in
his heart; he that backbites not with
his tongue, nor does evil to his
neighbor, nor takes up a reproach
against his neighbor; in whose eyes a
vile person is scorned; but he who
honors them that fear the Lord, who
swears to his own hurt, and changes
not, who puts not out his money to
usury nor takes a reward against the
innocent; he that does these things
shall never be moved.

What God has cleansed, call not common.

The word of God's grace is able to build
me up, and to give *me* an inheritance among
all them who are sanctified.

Mercy and truth are met together;
righteousness and peace have
kissed each other.

We ought to obey God rather than men.

Speak not evil of the ruler of your people.

The godly walk not in the counsel of the
ungodly, do not stand in the way of
sinners, do not sit in the seat of the
scornful, but delight in the law of the
Lord and meditate therein day and night.
The godly shall be like a tree planted by
the rivers of water, that brings forth
his fruit in his season; his leaf shall
not wither; and whatsoever he does shall
prosper. . . . The ungodly are like the chaff
which the wind drives away. . . . The Lord
knows the way of the righteous, but the
way of the ungodly shall perish.

The righteous Lord loves righteousness; His
countenance does behold the upright.

For Your Name's sake, O Lord, pardon my
iniquity; for it is great.

My defence is of God, Who saves the upright
in heart.

Study to show yourself approved unto God,
a workman who needs not be ashamed,
rightly dividing the word of truth. But
shun profane and vain babblings: for they
will increase to more ungodliness.

It is lawful to do well on the sabbath days.

It shall be well with the righteous: for
they shall eat the fruit of their doing.

It shall be ill to the wicked: for the reward
of his hands shall be given him.

Woe unto them that call evil good, and good
evil; that put darkness for light, and light
for darkness; that put bitter for sweet,
and sweet for bitter!

Let *your* light so shine before men,
that they may see *your* good works,
and glorify *your* Father in heaven.

If *you* break one of these least commandments
and teach men so, *you* shall be called the
least in the kingdom of heaven.

Provide things honest in the sight of all men.

Blessed are they which do hunger and thirst
after righteousness: for they shall be filled.

You are the salt of the earth . . .
the light of the world.

Judge not according to the appearance, but
judge righteous judgment.

As *I* have opportunity, *I* should do good to
all men, especially unto them who are of
the household of faith.

Because sentence against an evil work is not
executed speedily, therefore the heart of the
sons of men is fully set in them to do evil.. . .
It shall be well with them that fear God, . . .
but it shall not be well with the wicked.

The Lord blots out *my* transgressions for
His own sake, and will not remember *my* sins.

The Lord is good; His mercy is everlasting;
and His truth endures to all generations.

Whatsoever *I* sow, that shall *I* also reap.

God will bless them that fear the Lord,
both small and great.

A good man shows favor and lends: he will
guide his affairs with discretion. He shall
not be afraid of evil tidings: his heart
is fixed, trusting in the Lord.
He has given to the poor.

God has not dealt with *me* after *my* sins;
nor rewarded *me* according to *my* iniquities.

As the heaven is high above the earth, so
great is His mercy toward them that fear Him.

God visits the earth, and waters it.

The mercy of the Lord is from everlasting to
everlasting upon them that fear Him, and His
righteousness unto children's children; to
such as keep His covenant, and to those who
remember His commandments to do them.

My sins have withholden good things from *me*.

There is not a just man on earth,
that does good, and sins not.

Sin is the transgression of the law.

If *I* confess *my* sins, God is faithful and
just to forgive *me my* sins, and to cleanse
me from all unrighteousness.

Whoso rewards evil for good, evil shall not
depart from his house.

Fools make a mock at sin.

God causes the grass to grow for the cattle, and herb for the service of man: that he may bring forth food out of the earth; and wine that makes glad the heart of man, and oil to make his face to shine, and bread which strengthens man's heart.

The fear of the Lord is the beginning of wisdom: a good understanding have all they that do His commandments.

Blessed is the man that fears the Lord, that delights greatly in His commandments. His seed shall be mighty upon the earth: the generation of the upright shall be blessed. Wealth and riches shall be in his house.

If *I* provide not for *my* own, and specially for those of *my* own house, *I* have denied the faith and am worse than an infidel.

With the same measure that *I* mete, it shall be measured to *me* again.

He that is faithful in that which is least is faithful also in much: and he that is unjust in the least is unjust also in much.

To whom much is given, of him shall be much required.

I am the temple of God, and the Spirit of God dwells in *me*. If *I* defile the temple of God, He shall destroy *me*.

Grow in grace and in the knowledge of our Lord and Saviour Jesus Christ. To Him be glory both now and for ever. Amen.

Kindness

The Lord is good to all: and His tender
mercies are over all His works.

The Lord is merciful and gracious, slow to
anger, and plenteous in mercy.

Christ suffered for *me*, leaving *me* an example,
that *I* should follow in His steps.

Let us bear one another's burdens,
and so fulfil the law of Christ.

Create in *me* a clean heart, O God;
and renew a right spirit within *me*.

He who follows after righteousness and mercy
finds life, righteousness and honour.

Withhold not good from them to whom it is due,
when it is in the power of *your* hand to do it.

Cast out the beam from *your* own eye;
and *you* shall see clearly to cast out
the mote out of *your* brother's eye.

Strive not about words to no profit.

Love your enemies, do good to them that hate
you . . . that you may be children of your
Father which is in heaven: for He makes His
sun to shine on the evil and on the good, and
sends rain on the just and the unjust.

The Spirit Itself bears witness with my
spirit, that I am a child of God.

Be holy in all manner of conversation.

The wisdom that is from above is first pure,
then peaceable, gentle, and easy to be
intreated, full of mercy and good fruits,
without partiality, and without hypocrisy.

Strive not; but be gentle unto all men, apt
to teach, patient, in meekness instructing
those who oppose themselves.

Be still, and know that I am God.

A soft answer turns away wrath: but grievous
words stir up anger.

He who oppresses the poor reproaches
his Maker: but he who honors Him has
mercy on the poor.

Speak no evil of no man, be no brawler, but
gentle, showing all meekness to all men.

A righteous man regards the life of his
beast: but the tender mercies of the wicked
are cruel.

Be ye kind one to another, tenderhearted,
forgiving one another, even as God for
Christ's sake has forgiven you.

Avoid foolish and unlearned questions,
knowing they gender strife.

Let not the sun go down on *your* wrath.

A reproof means more to a wise man than a
hundred stripes to a fool.

All things are lawful for *me*, . . . but all
things edify not.

All things whatsoever *I* would that men should
do to *me*, *I* must do even so to them.

I am inexcusable if *I* judge another, . . . for *I*
that judge, do the same things.

God's mercy is on them who fear Him from
generation to generation.

The Lord daily loads *me* with benefits.

God shall give His angels charge over *me*,
to keep *me* in all *my* ways. They shall
bear *me* up in their hands, lest *I* dash *my*
foot against a stone.

O Lord, save *me* for Thy mercies' sake.

Love not the praise of men more than the
praise of God.

Favour is deceitful, and beauty is vain; but
a woman that fears the Lord, she shall be
praised. Give her of the fruit of her hands;
and let her own works praise her.

All the paths of the Lord are mercy and
truth unto such as keep His covenant
and His testimonies.

Cease from anger, and forsake wrath.

He that hath mercy on the poor, happy is he.

The pure in heart shall see God.

The merciful shall obtain mercy.

Suffer the little children to come unto Jesus: for of such is the kingdom of heaven.

It were better for *me* that a millstone were hanged about *my* neck, and that *I* were drowned in the bottom of the sea, than that *I* should offend a little one.

With the merciful God will show Himself merciful; with an upright man He will show Himself upright; with the pure He will show Himself pure.

It is more blessed to give than to receive.

I have been given exceeding great and precious promises, by which *I* may be a partaker of the divine nature.

If *I* say *I* abide in Jesus, *I* should walk even as He walked.

Father, forgive them;
for they know not what they do.

Goodness and mercy shall follow *me* all the days of *my* life: and *I* will dwell in the house of the Lord for ever.

The fruit of the Spirit is love, joy, peace, longsuffering, gentleness, goodness, faith, meekness and temperance.

Add to your faith virtue; and to virtue
knowledge; and to knowledge temperance;
and to temperance patience; and to patience
godliness; and to godliness brotherly
kindness; and to brotherly kindness charity.

If these things be in me, and abound,
I shall neither be barren nor unfruitful
in the knowledge of our Lord Jesus Christ.
If I lack these things, I am blind, and
cannot see afar off and have forgotten that
I was purged from my old sins.

Fear you not Me? says the Lord; will you not
tremble at My presence, Who has placed the
sand for the bound of the sea by a perpetual
decree, that it cannot pass it: and though
the waves thereof toss themselves, yet can
they not prevail; though they roar, yet
can they not pass over it?

Though the Lord be high, yet has He respect
unto the lowly.

Thus says the high and lofty One that
inhabits eternity, Whose name is Holy:
I dwell in the high and holy place, with
him also that is of a contrite and humble
spirit, to revive the spirit of the humble,
and to revive the heart of the contrite ones.

God is the judge: He puts down one and
sets up another.

When you pray, do not use vain repetitions . . .
for your Father knows what things you have
need of, before you ask Him.

Humble *yourself* in the sight of the Lord,
and He will lift *you* up.

God resists the proud, but gives grace
to the humble.

The Lord is gracious, and full of compassion;
slow to anger, and of great mercy.

The meek shall inherit the earth.

Humble *yourself* under the mighty hand of God
and He will exalt *you* in due time.

When *I* think *I* stand, *I* should take heed
lest *I* fall.

Every one of us shall give account of
himself to God. Let us not therefore judge
one another any more.

One day is with the Lord as a thousand years,
and a thousand years as one day.

When *you* give *your* alms, do not sound a
trumpet before you, as the hypocrites do . . .
that they may have glory from men.

The Lord lifts up the meek.

If *I* exalt *myself*, *I* shall be abased, if *I*
humble *myself*, *I* shall be exalted.

God knows *my* downsitting and *my* uprising,
He understands *my* thoughts afar off and is
acquainted with all *my* ways. There is not
a word in *my* tongue, but He knows it.

Boast not *yourself* of tomorrow; for *you* know
not what a day may bring forth.

God forgets not the cry of the humble.

The manifestation of the Spirit is given to
every man to profit withal. To one is given
by the Spirit the word of wisdom; to another
the word of knowledge by the same Spirit.
But all these work that one and the selfsame
Spirit, dividing to every man severally as
He will. As the body is one, and has many
members, and all the members of that one body,
being many, are one body: so also is Christ.

To every thing there is a season, and a
time to every purpose under the heaven.

I should say, If the Lord will, *I* shall
live, and do this, or that, for *I* know not
what shall be on the morrow.

God has chosen the foolish things of the
world to confound the wise; and God has
chosen the weak things of the world to
confound the things which are mighty;
and base things of the world, and things
which are despised, has God chosen, yea,
and things which are not, to bring to nought
things that are: that no flesh should glory
in His presence.

He that glories, let him glory in the Lord.

The Lord looks from heaven; He beholds
all the sons of men. From the place
of His habitation He looks upon all the
inhabitants of the earth. He fashions
their hearts alike; He considers all
their works.

God raises up the poor . . . that He may set
him with princes.

Every one that is proud in heart is an
abomination to the Lord.

The ways of man are before the eyes of
the Lord, and He ponders all his goings.

God gives grace to the lowly.

Submit *yourself* to every ordinance of man
for the Lord's sake, for so is the will of God.

For the Lord takes pleasure in His people:
He will beautify the meek with salvation.

Jesus came not to be ministered unto,
but to minister, and to give His life a
ransom for many.

Whosoever shall do the commandments and
teach them, he shall be called great in
the kingdom of heaven.

Be kindly affectioned one to another
with brotherly love; in honour
preferring one another.

There is no man that has power over the
spirit to retain the spirit; neither has he
power in the day of death.

By humility and the fear of the Lord are
riches, and honour, and life.

Be in the fear of the Lord all day long.

When pride comes, then comes shame: but with
the lowly is wisdom.

There is a way which seems right unto a man,
but the end thereof are the ways of death.

The natural man receives not the things of
the Spirit of God: for they are foolishness
unto him: neither can he know them, because
they are spiritually discerned.

God's thoughts are not *my* thoughts, neither
are *my* ways His ways, says the Lord.

Woe unto them that are wise in their own
eyes, and prudent in their own sight!

The entrance of God's word gives light; it
gives understanding to the simple.

Receive with meekness the engrafted word,
which is able to save *your* soul.

There are diversities of gifts, but the
same Spirit. There are differences of
administrations, but the same Lord.
There are diversities of operations, but
it is the same God Who works all in all.

I am the clay, and God is the potter; and
I am the work of His hand.

Let another man praise *thee* and not *thine* own
mouth; a stranger and not *thine* own lips.

Let the words of *my* mouth and the meditation
of *my* heart, be acceptable in Thy sight,
O Lord, *my* strength, and *my* redeemer.

Be subject one to another, and be clothed
with humility: for God resists the proud,
and gives grace to the humble.

If any man desire to be first, the same
shall be last of all, and servant of all.

Pride goeth before destruction, and an
haughty spirit before a fall.

He, who being often reproved and hardens
his neck, shall suddenly be destroyed, and
that without remedy.

God's goodness and forbearance and
longsuffering should lead *me* to repentance.

I brought nothing into this world, and
it is certain *I* shall carry nothing out.

Let not the wise man glory in his wisdom,
neither let the mighty man glory in his
might, let not the rich man glory in his
riches: but let him that glories glory in
this, that he understands and knows me,
that I am the Lord which exercise lovingkindness,
judgment, and righteousness, in the earth:
for in these things I delight, says the Lord.

The sacrifices of God are a broken spirit:
a broken and a contrite heart, O God,
You will not despise.

God's strength is made perfect in weakness.

The meek shall inherit the earth; and shall
delight themselves in the abundance of peace.

A meek and quiet spirit is of great price
in the sight of God.

If *I* think that *I* know anything, *I* know
nothing yet as *I* ought to know.

Wisdom

The fear of the Lord is the beginning of
wisdom; and the knowledge of the holy is
understanding.

Happy are they who find wisdom, and they who
get understanding. For the merchandise of it
is better than the merchandise of silver,
and the gain thereof than fine gold. She is
more precious than rubies: and all the
things I can desire are not to be compared
unto her. Length of days is in her right
hand; and in her left hand riches and honour.
Her ways are the ways of pleasantness, and
all her paths are peace. She is a tree of
life to them that lay hold upon her: and
happy is every one that retains her.

Riches and honour are with wisdom; yea,
durable riches and righteousness.

When wisdom enters into *my* heart, and
knowledge is pleasant to *my* soul; discretion
shall preserve *me*, understanding shall keep *me*.

How much better is it to get wisdom than
gold! and to get understanding rather
to be chosen than silver!

Wisdom is better than strength: nevertheless
the poor man's wisdom is despised, and his
words are not heard. The words of wise men
are heard in quiet more than the cry of him
that rules among fools. Wisdom is better
than weapons of war: but one sinner destroys
much good.

There is more hope for a fool than for a man
wise in his own conceits.

Understanding is a wellspring of life unto
him who has it.

Better is a poor and wise child than an old and
foolish king who will no more be admonished.

God gives to a man that is good in His
sight wisdom, and knowledge, and joy.

It is better for *me* to hear the rebuke of the
wise, than for *me* to hear the song of fools.

Every man also to whom God has given riches
and wealth, and has given him power to eat
thereof, and to take his portion, and to
rejoice in his labour; this is the gift of God.

There are those that make themselves rich,
and yet have nothing: there are those that
make themselves poor, yet have great riches.

A man's life consists not in the abundance
of things which he possesses.

Wealth gotten by vanity shall be diminished;
but he that gathers by labour shall increase.

He becomes poor that deals with a slack hand;
but the hand of the diligent makes rich.

I am a fool if I lay up treasure for *myself*,
and am not rich toward God.

Better is little with fear of the Lord than
great treasure and trouble therein.

Learn to be content in whatsoever
state *you* are.

Take no thought for *your* life, what ye shall
eat; neither for the body, what ye shall put
on. The life is more than meat, and the body
is more than raiment.

A good name is rather to be chosen than
great riches, and loving favour rather
than silver and gold.

Two are better than one; because they have a
good reward for their labor. If they fall,
the one will lift up his fellow: but woe to
him that is alone when he falls; for he hast not
another to help him up.

He who sows sparingly shall reap also
sparingly; and he who sows bountifully
shall reap also bountifully.

But rather seek the kingdom of God; and all
these things shall be added unto you.

So teach *me* to number *my* days, that I may
apply *my* heart unto wisdom.

The words of a wise man's mouth are gracious.

The fruit of the righteous is a tree of life;
and he that wins souls is wise.

A little that a righteous man has is better
than the riches of many wicked.

Blessed is the man unto whom the Lord
imputeth not iniquity, and in whose
spirit there is no guile.

Righteousness exalteth a nation; but sin is
a reproach to any people.

By much slothfulness the building decays;
and through the idleness of the hands the
house falls down.

Pleasant words are as a honeycomb, sweet to
the soul, and health to the bones.

A merry heart does good like a medicine.

The lips of the righteous feed many:
but fools die for want of wisdom.

The fear of the Lord is the instruction of
wisdom; and before honour is humility.

A word fitly spoken is like apples of gold
in pictures of silver.

Even so the tongue is a little member, and
boasts great things. Behold, how great a
matter a little fire kindles!

Even a fool, when he holds his peace, is
counted wise: and he who shuts his lips is
esteemed a man of understanding.

. . . Aged men be sober, grave, temperate,
sound in faith, in charity, in patience.
The aged women likewise . . . that they may
teach the young women to be sober, to love
their husbands, to love their children.

If *I* correct *my* son, he shall give *me* rest;
yea, he shall give delight unto *my* soul.

Children's children are the crown of old men;
and the glory of children are their fathers.

Children should hear the instruction
of their parents.

My son, give God your heart, and let your
eyes observe His ways.

A wise son maketh a glad father: but a
foolish son despiseth his mother.

Forsake not mercy and truth, . . . then shall
you find favor and good understanding in
the sight of God and man.

Abstain from all appearance of evil.

If *I* give, it shall be given to *me*, good
measure, pressed down, and shaken together
and running over.

A merry heart makes a cheerful countenance:
but by sorrow of the heart the spirit
is broken.

The judgments of the Lord are true and
righteous. More to be desired are they
than gold, yea, than much fine gold:
sweeter also than honey and the honeycomb.

I shall give account, in the day of
judgment, of every idle word *I* speak.

The Lord is near unto them that are of a
broken heart; and saves such as be of a
contrite spirit.

Man shall not live by bread alone, but by
every word that proceeds out of the mouth
of God.

He who covers a transgression seeks love;
but he who repeats a matter separates
very friends.

Hatred stirs up strifes: but love
covers all sins.

If the whole body were an eye, where were
the hearing? If the whole were hearing,
where were the smelling? . . . God has set
every member in the body as it has pleased
Him. . . . If one member suffers, all the
members suffer with it.

God has created all things, and for His
pleasure they are and were created.

Whatsoever things are true,
whatsoever things are honest,
whatsoever things are just,
whatsoever things are pure,
whatsoever things are lovely,
whatsoever things are of good report;
if there be any virtue,
and if there be any praise,
think on these things.

Faith

Who shall separate me from the love of Christ?
shall tribulation, or distress, or persecution,
or famine, or nakedness, or peril or sword?

Whosoever will, let him take of the water
of life freely.

Faith comes by hearing, and hearing by the word of God.

Faith is the substance of things hoped for, the
evidence of things not seen.

We trust in the living God, who is the Saviour
of all men, specially of those that believe.

Jesus Christ is the Son of the living God.

Jesus is the way, the truth, and the life:
no man comes unto the Father but by Him.

Christ Jesus came into the world to save sinners.

If I believe that Jesus is the Christ, I am born of God.

If I am born of God, I overcome the world; and the
victory that overcomes the world is my faith.

Other foundation can no man lay than that is laid, which is Jesus Christ.

We walk by faith, not by sight.

For *I* know whom *I* have believed, and am persuaded that He is able to keep that which *I* have committed to Him against that day.

The gospel of Christ is the power of God unto salvation to every one who believes.

Neither is there salvation in any other: for there is none other name under heaven given among men, whereby we must be saved.

God commends His love toward us, in that, while we were yet sinners, Christ died for us.

The wages of sin is death; but the gift of God is eternal life through Jesus Christ our Lord.

If *I* confess with *my* mouth the Lord Jesus, and believe in *my* heart that God has raised Him from the dead, *I* shall be saved.

With the heart man believes unto righteousness; and with the mouth confession is made unto salvation.

I am a child of God by faith in Christ Jesus.

By grace *I* am saved through faith; and that not of *myself*: it is a gift of God.

The just shall live by faith.

I shall not be afraid for the terror by night; nor for the arrow that flies by day; nor for the pestilence that walks in darkness; nor for the destruction that wastes at noonday.

I can do all things through Christ Who strengthens me.

My adversary, the devil, as a roaring lion walks about, seeking whom he may devour. Resist him steadfast in the faith.

Trust in the Lord and you shall not slide.

For this God is our God for ever and ever: He will be our guide even unto death.

Some trust in chariots, and some in horses: but I will remember the name of the Lord our God.

Our fathers trusted in God: they trusted and He delivered them.

God's commandment is that I should believe on the name of His Son Jesus Christ and love my brother. If I do this, God dwells in me and I in Him; and I know that He abides in me by the Spirit He has given me.

For as the heavens are higher than the earth, so are God's ways higher than my ways, and God's thoughts than my thoughts.

Try the spirits whether they are of God: because many false prophets are gone out into the world. I know the Spirit of God for every spirit that confesses Jesus Christ is come in the flesh is of God. Every spirit that confesses not that Jesus Christ is come in the flesh is not of God.

I am justified by faith without the deeds of the law.

The Spirit also helps my infirmities: for I know not what I should pray for as I ought: but the Spirit Itself makes intercession for me according to the will of God.

Let us hold fast the profession of our faith
without wavering; for He is faithful that promised.

If *I* deny the Son, *I* have not the Father: if *I*
acknowledge the Son, *I* have the Father also.

If *I* confess that Jesus is the Son of God, God
dwells in *me*, and *I* in God.

God has made the earth, and created man upon it.
His hands stretched out the heavens, and all their
host has He commanded.

I shall seek God, and find Him, when *I* search for
Him with all *my* heart.

Lord, teach *me* to pray.

If *I* abide in Him, and His words abide in *me*, *I*
shall ask what *I* will and it shall be done unto *me*.

The Lord is near unto all them that call upon
Him, to all that call upon Him in truth.

I ask, and receive not; because *I* ask amiss,
that *I* may consume it upon *my* lusts.

With God all things are possible.

Jesus is able to save them to the uttermost who
come unto God by Him, seeing He ever lives to
make intercession for them.

Cast not away *your* confidence, which has great
recompense of reward.

Ask in faith, nothing wavering. For he who wavers
is like a wave of the sea driven with the wind and
tossed. For let not that man think he shall receive
anything of the Lord.

According to my faith shall it be unto me.

All things whatsoever I ask in prayer, believing,
I shall receive.

Come boldly unto the throne of grace, and obtain
mercy, and find grace to help in time of need.

The effectual fervent prayer of a righteous man
avails much.

Ask God for wisdom, for He gives to all men
liberally, and upbraids not; and it shall
be given you.

What things soever I desire, when I pray, if I
believe that I receive them, I shall have them.

Without faith it is impossible to please God: for he
that comes to God must believe that He is, and that
He is a rewarder of them that diligently seek Him.

Pray without ceasing.

Fight the good fight of faith, lay hold on
eternal life.

Confess your faults one to another, and pray one
for another, and you shall be healed.

If afflicted, I should pray.

If I am sick, I should call for the elders of
the church; and let them pray over me, anointing
me with oil in the name of the Lord: and the
prayer of faith shall save me, and the Lord shall
raise me up; and if I have committed sins, they
shall be forgiven me.

God's house shall be called the house of prayer.

It shall come to pass, that before I call, God will
answer; and while I am yet speaking, He will hear.

Our Father which art in heaven,
Hallowed be Thy Name.
Thy Kingdom come.
Thy will be done in earth, as it is
in heaven.
Give us this day our daily bread.
And forgive us our debts, as we forgive
our debtors.
And lead us not into temptation, but
deliver us from evil.
For Thine is the kingdom, and the power,
and the glory, for ever.
Amen.

Continue in prayer, and watch in the same with
thanksgiving.

If my heart condemns me not, then have I confidence
toward God. And whatsoever I ask, I receive of Him,
because I keep His commandments, and do those things
which are pleasing in His sight.

And this is the confidence that I have in Him,
that, if I ask any thing according to His will,
He hears me: and if I know that He hears me,
whatsoever I ask, I know that I have the
petitions that I desired of Him.

Rejoice in hope; be patient in tribulation;
continue instant in prayer.

All things work together for good to them that
love God, to them who are the called according
to His purpose.

Cast your bread upon the waters: for you shall find it after many days.

Every word of God is pure: He is a shield to them that put their trust in Him.

Add not to God's words, lest He reprove you, and you be found a liar.

If I, being evil, know how to give good gifts to my children: how much more shall my heavenly Father give me the Holy Spirit if I ask Him.

The Lord is my rock, and my fortress, and my deliverer; my God, my strength, in Whom I will trust: my buckler, and the horn of my salvation, and my high tower.

Commit your way unto the Lord; and trust also in Him; and He shall bring it to pass.

Mercy shall encompass him who trusts in the Lord.

The eye of the Lord is upon them that fear Him, upon them that hope in His mercy; to deliver their soul from death, and to keep them alive in famine.

None that trust in God shall be desolate.

Be of good courage, and God shall strengthen your heart, all you that hope in the Lord.

The name of the Lord is a strong tower: the righteous runs into it, and is safe.

Trust in the Lord with all your heart; and lean not to your own understanding.

In all your ways acknowledge God, and He shall direct your paths.

Vain is the help of man; God will give *me* help
from trouble.

Cast *your* burden upon the Lord, and He shall
sustain *you*.

I will go in the strength of the Lord God!

I will hope continually, and will yet praise God
more and more.

It pleased the Father that in Christ should
all fulness dwell.

In Christ are hid all the treasures of wisdom
and knowledge.

By Christ were all things created, that are in
heaven, and that are in earth, visible and
invisible, whether they be thrones, or dominions,
or principalities, or powers: all things were
created by Him, and for Him: and He is before all
things, and by Him all things consist.

God was in Christ reconciling the world unto Himself.

God is a Spirit, and they that worship Him must
worship Him in spirit and in truth.

The kingdom of God is within *you*.

God is not the God of the dead, but of the living.

He who believes in the Son has everlasting life;
and he who believes not the Son shall not see life;
but the wrath of God abides on him.

I cannot be Jesus' disciple unless *I* forsake all—
father, mother, brother, sister, husband and even
be willing to give *my* own life.

Where two or three are gathered together in My name, there am I in the midst of them.

The Lord shall preserve my going out and my coming in from this time forth, and even for evermore.

Through God I shall do valiantly: for He it is that shall tread down my enemies.

I sought the Lord and He heard me, and delivered me from all my fears.

Blessed be God, Who has not turned away my prayer, nor His mercy from me.

God will fulfil the desire of them that fear Him: He also will hear their cry, and will save them.

He that believes and is baptized shall be saved; but he that believes not shall be damned.

Believe all things which are written in the law and in the prophets.

Prophecy came not in old time by the will of man: but holy men of God spoke as they were moved by the Holy Spirit.

Whatsoever things were written aforetime were written for our learning, that we through patience and comfort of the scriptures might have hope.

Open Thou my eyes that I may behold wondrous things out of Thy law.

Be ready always to give an answer to every man that asks you a reason of the hope that is in you.

If we hope for that we see not, then do we with patience wait for it.

He who turns away his ear from hearing the law,
even his prayer shall be abomination.

Take no thought for food or drink or clothes for
your heavenly Father knows *you* have need of
these things.

Seek first the kingdom of God and His righteousness;
and all these things shall be added to *you*.

We should make known the commandments to our
children; that the generation to come might know
them, even the children which should be born; who
should arise and declare them to their children:
that they might set their hope in God.

Train up a child in the way he should go; and
when he is old, he will not depart from it.

Jesus Christ is gone into heaven, and is on the
right hand of God; angels and authorities and
powers being made subject to Him.

All power is given to Jesus both in heaven and in earth.

Christ has once suffered for sins, the just for
the unjust, that He might bring us to God. . .

The fool has said in his heart,
there is no God.

Except the Lord build the house, they labour in
vain that build it: except the Lord keep the city,
the watchman wakes but in vain.

The trial of *my* faith is much more precious than
gold that perishes, though it be tried with fire,
and will give praise and honour and glory at the
appearing of Jesus Christ.

I must appear before the judgment seat of Christ; that
I may receive the things done in my body, according
to that I have done, whether it be good or bad.

The gates of hell shall not prevail against the Church.

The earth shall be full of the knowledge of the
Lord, as the waters cover the sea.

Although I have not seen Christ, I love Him; although
now I see Him not, yet I believe in Him and rejoice
with joy unspeakable.

In God I live, and move, and have my being.

Through faith I understand that the worlds were
framed by the word of God, so that things which
are seen were not made of things which do appear.

It is hard for those who trust in riches to enter
into the kingdom of God.

He that trusts in his riches shall fall: but the
righteous shall flourish as a branch.

I, according to God's promise look for new
heavens and a new earth, wherein dwells
righteousness.

I must search the scriptures; for in them I think
I have eternal life.

The angels are all ministering spirits sent forth
to minister for them who shall be heirs of salvation.

If I have faith as a grain of mustard seed,
nothing shall be impossible to me.

Here I have no continuing city, but I seek one
to come.

Commit *your* works unto the Lord, and *your* thoughts shall be established.

Seek ye the Lord while He may be found, call ye upon Him while He is near.

As the body without the spirit is dead, so faith without works is dead also.

It is appointed unto men once to die, but after this the judgment.

Jesus is the resurrection, and the life: he who believes in Him, though he were dead, yet shall he live: and whosoever lives and believes in Him shall never die.

I must continue in the faith grounded and settled, and be not moved away from the hope of the gospel.

Earnestly contend for the faith which was once delivered to the saints.

The end of *my* faith is the salvation of *my* soul.

This is life eternal, that *I* might know the only true God, and Jesus Christ, Whom He sent.

Now may the God of hope fill *me* with all joy and peace in believing, that *I* may abound in hope, through the power of the Holy Ghost.

The things which are seen are temporal; but the things which are not seen are eternal.

If *I* fight a good fight and keep the faith, there is laid up for *me* a crown of righteousness which the Lord, the righteous judge, shall give *me* at that day.

Promises

Holy Scripture is not the word of men, but it is
in truth, the word of God, which effectually
works in those who believe.

God's testimonies are my delight and my counsellors.

As the rain comes down, and the snow from heaven,
and returns not thither, but waters the earth,
and makes it bring forth and bud, that it may give
seed to the sower, and bread to the eater: so shall
God's word be that goes forth out of His mouth: it
shall not return unto Him void, but it shall
accomplish that which He pleases and it shall prosper
in the thing whereto He sent it.

Is not My word like as a fire? says the Lord;
and like a hammer that breaks the rock in pieces?

All scripture is given by inspiration of God, and
is profitable for doctrine, for reproof, for
correction, for instruction in righteousness; that
the man of God may be perfect, throughly furnished
unto all good works.

The words of the Lord are pure words: as silver
tried in a furnace of earth, purified seven times.

The word of God is not bound.

God's word is true from the beginning: and every
one of His righteous judgments endures for ever.

The Lord will perfect that which concerns me:
His mercy endures for ever.

The Lord is the first, and the Lord is the last;
and beside Him there is no God.

God's kingdom is an everlasting kingdom, and His
dominion endures throughout all generations.

Eye has not seen, nor ear heard, neither have
entered into the heart of man, the things which
God has prepared for them that love Him.

The Lord God is merciful and gracious,
longsuffering, and abundant in goodness and
truth, keeping mercy for thousands, forgiving
iniquity and transgression and sin.

Every good gift and every perfect gift is
from above, and comes down from the Father
of lights, with Whom is no variableness,
neither shadow of turning.

They that seek the Lord shall not want any good thing.

Trust in the Lord, and do good; so shall *you*
dwell in the land, and verily *you* shall be fed.

The Spirit of truth will guide *me* into all truth.

The holy scriptures are able to make *me* wise unto
salvation through faith which is in Christ Jesus.

The Lord is near to them that are of a broken heart;
and saves those who are of a contrite spirit.

. . . My presence shall go with thee,
and I will give thee rest.

They that mourn shall be comforted.

God will instruct *you* and teach *you* in the way which
you shall go: He will guide *you* with His eye.

Cast *your* burden upon the Lord, and He will sustain
you: He shall never suffer the righteous to be moved.

God shall supply all *my* need according to His
riches in glory by Christ Jesus.

Because *I* have made the Lord . . . *my* habitation;
there shall no evil befall *me*, neither shall
any plague come near *my* dwelling.

God will not suffer *my* foot to be moved; He that
keeps *me* will not slumber.

Draw nigh to God, and He will draw nigh to *you*.

The Lord does go before *you*; He will be with *you*,
He will not fail *you*, neither forsake *you*: fear not,
neither be dismayed.

I will lift up *mine* eyes unto the hills,
from whence cometh *my* help.

My help cometh from the Lord, which made heaven
and earth.

Fear not; for I am with *you*: be not dismayed; for
I am *your* God: I will strengthen *you*; yea, I will
help *you*; yea, I will uphold *you* with the right
hand of My righteousness.

If two agree on earth as touching any thing that they shall ask, it shall be done for them of our Father in heaven.

The Lord is *my* shepherd; *I* shall not want.

Whatsoever *I* shall ask in Jesus' name, that will He do, that the Father may be glorified in the Son.

I am the good shepherd, and know my sheep, and am known of mine.

He shall feed His flock like a shepherd: He shall gather the lambs with His arm.

Take heed how *you* hear: for whosoever has, to him shall be given; and he that has not, from him shall be taken even that which he seems to have.

. . . Be strong and of a good courage; be not afraid, be not dismayed: for the Lord your God is with *you*.

There shall be a resurrection of the dead, both of the just and the unjust.

The day of the Lord will come as a thief in the night; in the which the heavens shall pass away with a great noise, and the elements shall melt with fervent heat, the earth also and the works that are therein shall be burned up. Seeing then that all these things shall be dissolved, what manner of person ought *I* to be in all holy conversation and godliness, looking for and hasting unto the coming of the day of God.

When Christ, Who is *my* life, shall appear, then shall *I* also appear with Him in glory.

Dust shall return to the earth as it was; and the spirit shall return unto God Who gave it.

Jesus has gone to prepare a place for *me*.

Of that day and hour knows no man, no, not the angels of heaven, but our Father only. As in the days of Noah before the flood they were eating and drinking, marrying and giving in marriage, until the day Noah entered into the ark, and knew not until the flood came, and took them all away; so shall also the coming of the Son of man be. Then shall two be in the field; the one shall be taken, and the other left. . . . We should watch, for we know not what hour our Lord comes.

When Jesus shall be revealed from heaven with His mighty angels, He, in flaming fire, will take vengeance on them that obey not the gospel of our Lord Jesus Christ; He will punish with everlasting destruction from the presence of the Lord, and from the glory of His power.

The Lord Himself shall descend from heaven with a shout, with the voice of the archangel, and with the trump of God: and the dead in Christ shall rise first: then we who are alive and remain shall be caught up together with them in the clouds, to meet the Lord in the air: and so shall we ever be with the Lord. Wherefore comfort one another with these words.

Jesus will come again, and receive *me* unto Himself that where He is, *I* may be also.

If *I* keep Jesus' sayings, *I* shall never see death.

Christ, who is even at the right hand of God, makes intercession for *me*.

The Lord is Alpha and Omega, the beginning and the ending, Who is, and was, and is to come; it is He that lives, and was dead and is alive forevermore.

There is one God, and one mediator between God and men, the man Christ Jesus; who gave Himself a ransom for all.

Jesus was wounded for my transgressions, He was bruised for my iniquities: the chastisement of my peace was upon Him; and with His stripes I am healed.

If we walk in the light, as God is in the light, we have fellowship one with another, and the blood of Jesus Christ His Son cleanseth us from all sin.

In every thing I am enriched by Jesus Christ, in all utterance, and in all knowledge.

If I am faithful unto death, I shall receive a crown of life.

If I sin, I have an advocate with the Father, Jesus Christ the righteous: and He is the propitiation for my sins: and not for mine only, but also for the sins of the whole world.

The world passes away, and the lust thereof: but he that does the will of God abides for ever.

Believe on the Lord Jesus Christ, and you shall be saved, and your house.

Every man that has this hope in Christ purifies himself, even as Christ is pure.

Jesus says to us: he that believes in Me has everlasting life.

He that spared not His own Son, but delivered Him
up for us all, how shall He not with Him also
freely give us all things?

Whosoever therefore shall confess Me before men,
him will I confess also before My Father which
is in heaven.

Behold, the Lord's hand is not shortened, that
it cannot save; neither His ear heavy, that it
cannot hear.

For unto us a child is born, unto us a son is
given: and the government shall be upon his
shoulder: and his name shall be called Wonderful,
Counsellor, The mighty God, The everlasting
Father, The Prince of Peace.

If I drink of the water Jesus gives, I shall never
thirst; but the water that He gives shall be in me
a well of water springing up into everlasting life.

Jesus is able also to save them to the uttermost that
come to God by Him, seeing He ever lives to make
intercession for them.

Jesus is the resurrection, and the life:
he that believes in Him, though he were
dead, yet shall he live.

Jesus said: My sheep hear my voice; and I know them,
and they follow Me: and I give unto them eternal
life; and they shall never perish, neither shall any
man pluck them out of My hand.

Jesus said: I am the light of the world: he that
follows Me shall not walk in darkness, but shall
have the light of life.

I declare unto you the gospel . . . by which also you
are saved, . . . how that Christ died for our sins according
to the scriptures; and that He was buried, and that
He rose again the third day according to the scriptures.

If Christ be not raised, your faith is vain; you are
yet in your sins. Then they also which are fallen
asleep in Christ are perished. If in this life only
we have hope in Christ, we are of all men most
miserable. But now is Christ risen from the dead,
and become the firstfruits of them that slept.

He that believes on the Son has everlasting life.

But as many as receive Jesus, to them He gives
power to become the sons of God, even to them
that believe on His name.

If God be for me, who can be against me?

Ask, and it shall be given you; seek, and you shall
find; knock, and it shall be opened to you.

The Lord is able to keep me from falling, and to
present me faultless before the presence of His
glory with exceeding joy. To the only wise God
our Saviour, be glory and majesty, dominion and
power, both now and ever.

Behold, I stand at the door, and knock: if any man
hear My voice, and open the door, I will come in to
him, and will sup with him, and he with Me.

The Lord bless thee, and keep thee:
The Lord make His face shine upon thee, and be
gracious unto thee:
The Lord lift up His countenance upon thee, and
give thee peace.

Set in Melior, a typeface
designed by Hermann Zapf.

Designed and illustrated by
Gordon Brown.